Quick & Easy Autism Cookbook

Dawn Lucan

Quick & Easy Autism Cookbook

Copyright © 2010-2011 by Dawn Lucan

All rights reserved. No part of this book may be used or reproduced in any manner whatsoever without written permission except in the case of brief quotations embodied in critical studies and reviews.

ISBN 978-0-557-55133-0

Library of Congress Cataloging in Publication Data

Dawn Lucan

Quick & Easy Autism Cookbook

1. Healthy Diet 2. Autism Cookbook 3. Persuasive Developmental Disorder Cookbook 4. Asperger Syndrome Cookbook 6. Special Needs Parenting

To my brother, you inspire me every day.

To my mother, thank you for helping me become who I am.

To my friends, you inspire me every day.

Foreword

I am a busy person and on the go often. I participate in sports. I read books. I go to the movies. I go to the beach. I write books. I am a good cook. I can budget my own money. I have many good friends from over the years. I love to travel across the country. I can clean my own place. I can organize my own things. I can manage my own money. I can organize my own time well. I am an adult diagnosed with Asperger Syndrome more than a decade ago as an adult.

I will be the first to admit that I have really busy days. It is hard to get in a good and quick healthy meal at times.

It is harder for me since I am a special diet. Throughout this cookbook, I will give general mixes for you to use. It is your choice on which mix package you can use. I have adapted over time many different mixes over time. It turned out great each time for me and my family.

The tricks that I have used throughout this cookbook are ones that my own Mother used while I was growing up. There is nothing really complicated to make any mixture healthy without spending a fortune on your food budget.

Since I became an adult on a budget for a time, I learned many different ways to save money on my food budget. I use a variety of different ways to save money each month on it. I am proud that I can budget my own money wisely.

I am not a professional cook. I am not a registered dietician. I did take a home economics cooking course in high school. I had a really great teacher who inspired us all. I am just simply me who was diagnosed with Asperger Syndrome more than a decade before now.

I have included two book exerts at the end of the book. It should be very useful or helpful in understanding Autism or Asperger's Syndrome.

Enjoy!

Table of Contents

Introduction 1

Quick Breakfasts 5

Quick and Easy Meal Ideas 9

Healthy Snacks 19

Easy Baking 27

Beverages 35

Important Website Resources 43

Introduction

For as long as I can remember, I have been different. I did not know how or why. I just knew that I behaved and sounded different than the other neighborhood kids. Later, it included my classmates in school.

It was not until my Father's fiancé later third wife encouraged me to search for answers. I was diagnosed for the longest time with Attention Deficit Hyperactive Disorder with the inattentive form. It was a diagnosis given to me during my preteen years. I also had the diagnosis of being learning disabled.

I was young when a neighbor noticed that I was developing differently from the other children. This happened during the early 1970s. I started receiving help from professionals from then on with the characteristics of my unknown disability.

I had received help during my school years in the form of Special Education. I had attended small classes from the time I entered first grade. I graduated from high school receiving help in the resource classroom room setting.

I did great academically. I did not struggle in the resource room as much. I did struggle some with the mainstream classroom. It was entirely not academic in nature. I had a number of struggles with my fine motor skills. I could not handle intensive writing classes well. I got overwhelmed at times with it.

I had a major difficulty with individuals teasing me almost throughout my school years. There were a couple of years when I was not teased by someone. My bullies primarily focused on my appearance which meant body and clothing.

I had trouble finding a group of friends to associate with during school hours. Most individuals ignored me. I did find a helpful group of friends during my senior year of high school when I joined a school band as a manager.

I dreamed of being a teacher from a young age. I played with my few friends about being a teacher. I always thought it was possible.

I did attend college as an education major. I did great academic wise. I still had some problems social wise. I did not know how to fit in with any campus crowd just like I did during my school years. I did participate with some clubs though. I did not graduate with teacher certification.

I did work after graduation. It took a bit of work since I did not interview well in person. I could read very little body language.

There were two attempts at getting me help during my childhood. I did have a little success with the psychological therapy during my childhood. I did receive a diagnosis of Attention Deficit Hyperactive

Disorder. The diagnosis was later discarded in 1996 when I was diagnosed with a form of Mild Autism.

After moving to Michigan in 1996, I became interested in finding a diagnosis that fit me. It came after being encouraged by my future step mother to search for one. She worked as a social worker who worked at an adult day care.

I first tried a psychiatrist for a diagnosis. I spent a number of weeks seeing him. It was covered by my insurance. He gave me medication for anxiety. However, he did not find a cause for my anxiety.

After a while, my father and future step mother decided to try a second place. It was a nonprofit which serviced both Autistic and developmentally disabled adults.

We believed it would work in finding a diagnosis. We thought they knew all levels of Autism since they worked with lower functioning adults. The place seemed to be perfect fit in finding the services needed to help me at the time.

The intake worker was fantastic. He seemed to notice my difficulties very well. The evaluation went well. However, it was difficult getting the results. The person had a difficult time believing I was on the Autism spectrum. The results were disheartening.

I decided to research before trying to get an evaluation. I heard that a major state university had an Autism Department. I decided to try there. I had no luck in finding it. I tried the university's telephone system and the university's website.

I decided to try the Autism Society located within the state for my next attempt. I talked to someone over the telephone, and I was referred to two different doctors in my county.

After talking to both places, I decided to go with one place. My health insurance was not taken there. It did not bother me at all. I just wanted an accurate diagnosis. I had to wait several months before I could be seen. It worked! I was accurately diagnosed with Mild Autism for the first time in my entire life.

I felt relieved once I had my diagnosis. I finally had the answers that I had been searching for consciously or unconsciously for years. It was all thanks to a family member who encouraged me to search for answers. I felt like I had some closure in my life when it came to finding answers.

Quick Breakfasts

Chocolate Chip Pancakes

Pancake Mix
2 tablespoons of apple puree
2 tablespoons of banana puree
¼ cup of chocolate chips

Prepare the pancake mix as as prepared by the package in a bowl. Mix in the apple puree and chocolate chips. Cook the pancakes as directed by the box. Serve!

My Favorite Muffins

1 package of muffin mix (any flavor)
2 tablespoons applesauce
2 tablespoons of peach puree

Prepare the muffin mix as directed on the package. Mix in the applesauce. Bake as directed on the muffin mix box. Serve!

Very Berry Oatmeal

1 individual serving of oatmeal (can be flavored)
1 teaspoon of applesauce
6 blueberries washed and drained
4 strawberries washed and drained

Prepare the oatmeal according to package. Mix into the oatmeal the applesauce. Cut up the strawberries. Add the blueberries and strawberries. Serve.

Serves 1

Quick and Easy Meal Ideas

Better BBQ Sauce

½ cup of your favorite BBQ Sauce
4 tablespoons of pureed beats
2 tablespoons of tomato paste
2 tablespoons of pureed carrots
2 tablespoons of honey

Place all ingredients into a mixing bowl. Mix it until well combined. Refrigerate remaining unused recipe. Serve!

Franks and Beans

1 can of your favorite baked beans
4 diced hot dogs
2 tablespoons of pureed beets
2 tablespoons of spaghetti sauce
2 tablespoons of pureed yams

Add all ingredients into a cooking pot. Cook according to the baked beans can. Stir well throughout cooking. Serve!

Hamburgers

1 pound of hamburger
2 tablespoons of pureed carrots
2 tablespoons of tomato paste
2 tablespoons of pureed butter beans

Combine all ingredients into a mixing bowl. Mix well. Form into four different even patties. Cook until you have it done the way you like it. Serve!

Serves 4

Healthy Meatballs

1 pound of hamburger
¼ cup of cornmeal
¼ cup of cooked rice
2 tablespoons of pureed butter beans
2 tablespoons of pureed beats
2 tablespoons of grated cheese

Combine all ingredients into a mixing bowl. Form into balls. Cook until brown. Add spaghetti sauce. Serve on top of spaghetti noodles. Serve!

Healthy Stuffing

1 box of your favorite stuffing mix
1 cup of creamed corn
2 tablespoons of pureed butter beans
2 tablespoons of applesauce
2 tablespoons of pureed wax beans
2 tablespoons of pureed peaches

Prepare the stuffing according to the box's directions. Stir in the remaining ingredients. Serve!

Macaroni and Cheese

1 box of your favorite macaroni and cheese
4 tablespoons of pureed butter beans
4 tablespoons of pureed chick peas

Cook and prepare the macaroni and cheese according to the box. Drain the water. Add the remaining ingredients. Mix well. Serve!

Mashed Potatoes

1 box of mashed potatoes
¼ cup of pureed butter beans
¼ cup of pureed cauliflower
¼ cup of pureed chick peas

Prepare the mashed potatoes according to the recipe on the box. Add in the remaining ingredients. Mix until well combined. Serve!

Tacos

1 box of complete taco meal (tacos and seasoning)
2 tablespoons of pureed beats
2 tablespoons of tomato paste
2 tablespoons of pureed butter beans

Prepare the tacos according to the package's directions. Stir in the beats, tomato paste, and butter beans. Serve!

Wise Ranch Dipping Sauce

¼ cup of your favorite ranch salad dressing
4 tablespoons of plain yogurt
2 tablespoons of pureed butter beans
2 tablespoons of pureed chick peas

Combine all ingredients into a mixing bowl. Mix until well combined. Store in the refrigerator any remaining leftover dip. Serve!

Wonderful Spaghetti Sauce

1 can or bottle of your favorite spaghetti sauce
2 tablespoons of pureed beets
4 tablespoons of pureed carrots
2 tablespoons of pureed butter beans

Cook the spaghetti sauce as directed. Mix in the remaining ingredients. Serve!

Healthy Snacks

Cheesy Nacho Dip

1 cup of cheddar cheese dip
¼ cup of plain yogurt
2 tablespoons of pureed chick peas
2 tablespoons of butter beans
2 tablespoons of nutrition powder
2 teapoons of chili powder

Place all ingredients into a mixing bowl. Mix well together. Serve with corn tortilla chips!

Chomp Cereal Mix

2 cups of your favorite cereal
2 cups of another of your favorite cereals
¼ cup of shredded coconut
¼ of raisins
¼ cup of peanut butter chips
¼ cup of chocolate chips
1/8 cup of of plain yogurt
2 tablespoons of honey

Mix all ingredients into a mixing bowl. Mix well. Serve!

Easy Applesauce

2 cups of applesauce
2 tablespoons of pear puree
2 tablespoons of peach puree
2 tablespoons of nutritional supplement

Place all ingredients in a bowl and mix well until combined. Serve!

Serves 4

Fruity Jello

1 package of jello
Grape Juice

Prepare the jello according to the box except for replacing the water for the grape juice. Mix well. Chill according to the package. Serve!

Icy Fruit Cubes

¼ cup grape juice
2 tablespoons of apple juice
2 tablespoons of cherry juice
2 tablespoons of pineapple juice

Place all ingredients into a mixing bowl. Mix well. Fill up each slot in the ice cube tray. Freeze overnight. Serve!

Great for punch bowls. Summer beverages.

Popcorn Lovers Delight Mix

1 package of your favorite microwave popcorn
4 tablespoons of plain yogurt
¼ cup of raisins
¼ cup of chocolate chips
¼ cup of shredded coconut

Prepare the popcorn according to the package. Pour the popcorn into the bowl. Add the remaining ingredients. Mix well. Serve!

Salsa Dip

1 jar of your favorite salsa
2 tablespoons of pureed carrots
2 tablespoons of pureed kidney beans
2 tablespoons of tomato paste
2 tablespoons of butter beans

Place all ingredients into a mixing bowl. Mix until well combined. Serve with tortilla or potato chips.

Yogurt Delight

1 cup of yogurt of any flavor
6 blueberries washed and drained
6 strawberries washed and drained
2 tablespoons of apple puree
2 tablespoons of peach puree
2 tablespoons of cherry puree
2 tablespoons of nutritional supplement

Place all ingredients into the blender. Blend for 3 minutes. Serve!

Serves 2

Easy Baking

Biscuits

Bisquick Baking Mix
1 teaspoon of applesauce
1 teaspoon of honey

Prepare according to the directions on the box. Mix in the applesauce and honey. Bake according to the directions on the box. Serve!

Bread

1 quick ready bread mix box
2 tablespoons peach puree
2 tablespoons applesauce
2 tablespoons pear puree
2 tablespoons banana puree

Prepare the bread mix as directed on the mix box. Mix in the peaches, applesauce, and pear. Bake as directed on the box. Serve!

Brownies

1 box of brownie mix (your favorite flavor)
2 tablespoons of applesauce
2 tablespoons of pear puree
2 tablespoons of peach puree

Prepare the brownie mix according to the applesauce recipe on the box. Mix in the pears and the peaches. Bake as directed. Serve!

Cake

1 box of your favorite cake mix
2 tablespoons of peach puree
2 tablespoons of pear puree

Prepare the cake mix according to the applesauce recipe variant on the box. Mix in the peaches and pears. Bake according to the box. Serve!

Chocolate Chip Dream Cookies

1 package of chocolate chip cookies
2 tablespoons of oatmeal
1 teaspoon of pureed apple
1 teaspoon of pureed apricot

Prepare the cookie mixture according to the package. Add the remaining ingredients into the mixture. Bake according to the directions on the package. Serve!

Coffee Cake

1 box of your favorite coffee cake
Applesauce
2 tablespoons of pureed pears
2 tablespoons of pureed apricots
2 tablespoons of pureed peaches

Follow the applesauce recipe listed on the box. Mix in the remaining ingredients. Bake according to the box's directions. Serve!

Lemony Treat Bars

1 box of Lemon Bars Mix
1 lemon
2 tablespoons of shredded coconut
2 tablespoons of pureed apples
2 tablespoons of pureed peaches

Prepare according to the recipe on the box. Squeeze the lemon into the bowl containing the mixture. Mix in the remaining ingredients into the mixture. Bake according to the package. Serve!

Sugar Cookies

1 package of sugar cookie mix
1 teaspoon of pureed apples
2 tablespoons of shredded coconut

Prepare the sugar cookie mixture according to the package. Add the apples to the mixture and stir well. Prepare the cookies on the cookie tray according to the directions on the box. Sprinkle the coconut on top of the cookies. Bake according to the directions on the package. Serve!

Beverages

Best Milkshake Ever

1 cup milk
2 scoops your favorite flavor of ice cream
2 tablespoons of chocolate syrup
1 tablespoon of blueberry juice
2 tablespoons of nutritional supplement

Place all ingredients into the blender. Set the blender on the blender setting for three minutes. Pour into two tall glasses. Serve!

                                                                                    Serves 2

Chocolate Milk

2 cups of milk
2 tablespoons of pear puree
2 tablespoons of apple puree
2 tablespoons of nutritional supplement

Place all ingredients into the blender. Set the blender on the blender setting for three minutes. Pour into two tall glasses. Serve!

Serves 2

Chocolate Soda

¾ cup of seltzer water
2 tablespoons of chocolate syrup
1 tablespoon of apple juice
1 tablespoon of blueberry juice

Put all ingredients into a glass. Stir until well combined about 2 minutes. Serve!

Serves 1

Grape Smoothie

1 cup of grape juice
¼ cup orange juice
¼ cup of pineapple juice
1 tablespoon of blueberry juice
12 blueberries washed and drained
2 tablespoons of nutritional powder
4 nice cubes

Place all ingredients in the blender. Blend for three minutes. Pour into two tall glasses. Serve!

Serves 2

Orange Juice Smoothie

1 cup of orange juice
½ cup of apple juice
1 banana
2 tablespoons of apple puree
2 tablespoons of pear puree
1 tablespoon of blueberry juice
2 tablespoons of nutritional supplement
4 cubes of ice

Place all ingredients into the blender. Set the blender on the blender setting for three minutes. Pour into two tall glasses. Serve!

Serves 2

Peaches and Cream Smoothie

2 cups of milk
¼ cup of peach puree
2 tablespoons of pear puree
2 tablespoons of nutritional powder

Place all ingredients into the blender. Set the blender on the blender setting for three minutes. Pour into two tall glasses. Serve!

Serves 2

Real Lemonade

4 cups of water
2 cups of seltzer water
¼ cup of lemon juice
1/3 cup of sugar
¼ cup of cherry juice
¼ cup of blueberry juice
8 cubes of ice

Mix all ingredients together into a pitcher. Serve!

Very Berry Smoothie

1 cup of apple juice
12 Blueberries washed and drained
6 Strawberries washed, cut and drained
12 Blackberries washed and drained
¼ cup of blueberry juice
2 tablespoons of nutritional supplement
4 ice cubs

Place all ingredients into a blender. Set the blender on the blend setting for three minutes or until all ingredients are mixed in. Pour into two glasses. Serve!

Serves 2

Important Website Resources

I have included a list of websites that I have found useful over the years. I refer people all the time to them. I have no professional association with their organization, company, or website.

Autism Society: www.autism-society.org
Boy Scouts of America: www.scouting.org
Cafemom: www.cafemom.com
Campfire USA: www.campfire.org
Easter Seals: www.easterseals.org
Generation Rescue: www.generationrescue.org
Girl Scouts of America: www.girlscouts.org
Goodwill Industries: www.goodwill.org
Special Olympics: www.specialolympics.org
TheARC: www.thearc.org
Variety Club: www.usvariety.org
VerySpecialArts: www.vsarts.org
WebMd: www.webmd.com
Wrightslaw: www.wrightslaw.com
YMCA: www.ymca.net

Sneak Preview of Practical Autism Manual

You have spent many sleepless nights trying to discover what is wrong or different about your child. You have finally got the diagnosis. Where do you go from here after receiving it?

The biggest thing to remember is that your child has not changed at all. The only thing that has changed is that there is a name to your child's problems that he or she is facing on a regular basis. The other thing is that you are not alone in facing these problems.

Remember your child still has the same gifts given to him or her before she received the diagnosis. They have a talent in something which will develop in time just like any other child.

Your child will always have some sort of interest. It sort of takes the form of a fixation of interest. They will want to learn everything they can about it. At times, they will even want to observe it in more detail. This parenting and personality trait can work to your advantage at times with things.

Consistency will benefit your child in more ways than one. Many on the Autism spectrum including Mild Autism prefer having consistency in their lives. It could be a predictable schedule or even a checklist. Having a large task broken down into its smaller parts can help your child, too.

You can utilize it as enrichment material with learning a new educational concept. For example, you can turn it into solving word problems if they are struggling to learn it. It will make the child want to learn even more about it.

Your child loves to research about their current fixation in many different ways. It can be used as an advantage to get them to read more about it. The library becomes your ally in finding books about it.

I recommend taking a deep breath because things can improve with the right help. He or she may not always be the perfect child every moment of the day. However, his or her coping mechanisms for dealing with their disability can improve.

Your significant other or spouse can help or hinder your child in developing. The trick is to learn their unique abilities in order to help you in ways that are beneficial to help your disabled child.

Your spouse or significant other may or may not accept the diagnosis right away if ever. His or her response to the diagnosis may take one of several different forms.

They may want to place the blame on you for something out of your control. Remind them that blaming someone for genetics does not help the child. You can try to encourage them to help with things to encourage personal growth in the child. Show your spouse or significant other how they can help you with them. It may take time before this happens.

The hardest one to deal with is the denial of the problem. It could stem from one of several different reasons. One reason could be that they could have it undiagnosed. A different reason could be that they believe the child is acting just like a normal child.

Find little things for them to help with on a regular basis to help you. Do it without nagging about it. It does not have to be child related. It could be helping around the house. Share the impact which it could have for him or her in the future if done. For example, it could be more energy for watching a favorite television show you both enjoy watching together.

Your spouse or significant other might have the diagnosis in himself or herself. It could be diagnosed or undiagnosed. If undiagnosed, the problem could have been ignored for years. This denial can have a huge impact on their parenting of the child.

If the parent is showing signs of Mild Autism, there is help for you. Their denials can take a couple of forms. However, you can also use their best qualities to help you help your Autistic child.

Utilize their strengths in assisting you. For example, if they are good at computers, they can share what they have learned over time. Their fixations on a subject can be a huge asset at times when researching a particular subject to help your disabled child.

Encourage him or her to find help some form of help. They can become a role model for the child in seeking help.

Encourage role modeling behavior. Have them show positive attributes in front of the child. Those individuals with Mild Autism learn by mimicking sometimes. You can give them some signal when they are doing great or correct when necessary on their behavior.

The second type is avoidance and the belief it is just a developmental stage that will vanish with maturity. It is a hard sell. The person might believe it based on the assumption every child is like it at one point or another in his or her lifetime.

Someone could be pressuring them on the child being normal. It could be a family member, medical professional, or even a teacher. The person could believe give it a little time, and the child will grow in maturity. You are arguing against two or more people in this case.

Avoidance could create problems with consistency with therapeutic and parenting methods. The reason is there is no agreement with the parenting method between the parents. It could create confusion for the child in regards to the schedule or expectations.

Avoidance approach can sometimes create worse behavior problems in your child. The mixed signals could create confusion with the child on their expectations. As a result, they do not learn the proper social and behavioral expectations for a social situation or interaction.

The third type is the fix it mode. They are trying to find a quick fix to help your child overcome his or her disability. He or she might research possible cures on the web or read books on it. These approaches may or may not work.

You can actually work with this kind of acceptance in a team parenting approach. However, there might be a problem or two which might occur from time to time due to a lack of communication between the two of you on things.

You can utilize him or her to research the latest parenting or educational methods. There are new books, magazines, and websites which come out on a regular basis on a variety of topics. The key is to get them to share their findings with you before implementing them. Otherwise, you could find them undermining your decisions regarding your child.

The trick is to remind them to be patient during the process because any new method needs time to work. It does not matter if it is a new parenting method or therapy. It takes time and patience to implement and work effectively.

In addition, you need to remind them about it being a team effort. If you two do not work as a team, the new method will not work. Neither one should undermine the other.

Undermining your partner and team member can take the form of correcting them in front of the child. Your corrections should be done in private. Consistency is the key to the new method taking hold and working with your child when it comes to new utilizing new parenting methods.

If a new treatment method is located, you need to consult or need to encourage approaching the doctor or therapist. They know if the treatment will work against any current medical treatment. There is a computer system which will help him judge if it will be harmful to your child.

Acceptance is the final parenting mode. They work with you on parenting and punishment mode. They provide assistance in whichever way that helps you such as handling appointments. They make it a true team effort for the benefit of the child.

Is there any common advice to follow in making my quality of life easier with this disability? Yes, there are things you can do to improve your quality of life.

Suggest tasks to them to help you with taking care of the child. Do not use a nag and instead use a helpful tone. Show appreciation for their help before, during and after the task. This will encourage them to help more often.

There are things you can do no matter how cooperative the other parent is with you. It can help ease the parenting tension.

Take time for yourselves no matter what. Raising a disabled child is a difficult task. It could be individual or couples time. It gives you a chance to recharge your mental batteries.

Gently remind yourself there will always be a difference of opinions on things. Even among parents have the same belief and parenting system, there will always be differences. The trick is how both of you handle the difference of opinions on things.

Join a support group. The local hospital or school social worker will have a list of them. They are great when you are facing a problem related to the disability. In addition, there are people with varying degrees of experience with it.

Keep a diary of things related to his disability. It could be of medical, personal, and educational stuff. You have no idea when it would come in handy in the future.

Never stop learning or researching about the disability. There is always new research material coming out. Some of it could help you with raising your child. The local intermediate unit or college library would have access to these research journals. In addition, some of these journals can be located on the web for free.

Put time aside each day to communicate with each other. Select a time of day that works for both of you. It could be about any issue or even your day. It could be as little as sharing accomplishments or problems. The main thing is not to be judgmental. Communication is important no matter what to making a relationship work.

Remember to give verbal or written praise for their accomplishments no matter how big or small. Positive feedback can make a great impact on him or her on how they view and handle things.

If you have a normal developing child, make time for him or her on a regular basis. When you have a disabled child, it is really easy to focus more on the disabled child.

There is no single approach in handling a child with Mild Autism. The main thing is to remember is that your child is more than their disability. You are not helpless in helping them become a productive adult. It does not have to cost any money.

In later chapters, you will learn some skills that I found important in helping your child at home, school, and in your local community.

Sneak Preview of Preschool Memories of My Childhood

I take the school bus to school. I ride it every morning. I ride the bus every afternoon. It picks me up from my house.

My brother goes to school before me. He walks to the corner to catch his school bus.

I get dressed in the morning. I put on my shirt. I put on my underwear. I put on my pants. I put on my socks. I put on my shoes. Mommy ties my shoe laces for me.

It comes after I eat breakfast. I eat cereal with milk. I eat toast with butter and jelly. I drink orange juice. I drink milk.

Mommy packs my lunch while I eat breakfast. She packs my lunch in my lunch box.

Four things go into my lunch box. She packs me a sandwich. She packs me potato chips. She packs me an apple. She packs me a juice box. I love eating my lunch at school.

I climb the stairs after breakfast. I go to the bathroom. I have to brush my teeth.

I brush my teeth in front of the mirror. I brush my top teeth. I brush my bottom teeth. I rinse my mouth of tooth paste.

I leave the bathroom. I go down the stairs. My backpack is by the door. I am almost ready for the school bus.

Mommy is waiting by the front door. She is looking out the window. She is waiting for the school bus to come.

I have two more things to do. I put on my jacket. I put on my backpack.

She hears me walking down the stairs. She turns to look at me. She begins to smile at me. I think she is happy with me.

She checks to see if I am dressed fine. She checks to see if my shoes are on the right feet. She looks to see if my shirt is on right. She gives me a thumbs up. Everything looks perfect.

We hear the school bus honking. It lets us know the bus is here. It is parked in our drive way.

Mommy opens our door. She walks outside. I walk outside after her. She closes the door.

I hold my Mommy's hand. I have to when we go out. She needs my hand. She says it makes her happy. I am happy, too!

We start walking down the path. It will take us to the drive way. It is where the school bus is waiting for me.

The school bus door opens. I see my bus driver waiting for me. I am so happy to see her. I love going to school!

The bus driver gets out of the bus. She is holding a small stool. She places the stool on the ground. It is in front of the stairs.

It is three steps to get onto the bus. I climb up each step. It is very easy to get onto the bus.

The school bus driver picks up the stool. She climbs up the three steps. She places the stool next to the steering wheel.

I walk down the bus aisle. I go sit in my seat. I see most of my friends are on the bus. I have one more friend to see. He gets on the bus after me. I sit quietly.

The school bus driver sits in her seat. She starts the school bus. She starts driving the bus.

The school bus driver begins driving down the road. She stops at a house and picks up someone.

The boy gets on the bus. He sits in his seat. The school bus driver sits in her seat.

The driver starts the school bus. The bus gets on the road again. We are almost at school. Everyone is on board.

The school bus turns into the school parking lot. The bus driver parks the bus. She opens the door. She grabs the stool. She gets out of the bus. She places the stool on the ground.

I get off of my seat. I start walking down the aisle. I go down the stairs. I step onto the stool. I step onto the ground.

I will not hit a classmate. A classmate will not hit me.

My teacher is waiting for me. She grasps my hand. We start walking toward the school.

My teacher and I reach the door. My teacher opens the door. I walk through the door. My teacher walks through the door.

I walk down the hallway with my teacher. We stop at our classroom door. My teacher opens the door. We walk through the door into the classroom.

I love talking to people. I enjoy listening to people. People are so much fun to learn from. People are so much fun to listen to.

I talk to a person. I share an idea. I share a problem. I share a joke.

Mommy will respond to what I say. She will share her idea. She will share her solution. She will laugh. She will share a joke with me.

I will respond back to Mommy. I will share my response with Mommy. I will laugh with Mommy. I will share another joke with Mommy.

Mommy will respond to what I say. She will share her idea. She will share her solution. She will laugh. She will share a joke with me.

I will respond back to Mommy. I will share my response with Mommy. I will laugh with Mommy. I will share another joke with Mommy.

I will listen to Mommy. Mommy will listen to me. I love listening to Mommy!

I love talking with Mommy! She is so much fun to talk to. She is so much fun to share a joke with her!

I am waiting in line. I am waiting for something to happen. I know it will be for something good. I know that waiting is good.

The wait will be done soon. The line has an end. The end is where I get something good. I like waiting for something good!

Everyone has their place in line. I hate it when someone new gets in front of me. I love waiting in line!

Someone ahead in line moves forward a step. I move forward a step in line.

I wait in line in the school cafeteria. I wait in line at the amusement park. I wait in line at the county fair. I wait in line at the grocery store.

I wait by myself in line. I wait with Mommy in line. I wait with my brother in line. Everyone waits in line!

I will not hit someone. My classmate will not hit me.

I will leave the line when I get something good. I will walk to my next place. I will feel happy!

About the Author

Dawn Lucan is a disabled freelance writer who lives on the East Coast. She has written Simply Gluten Free Cooking and Practical Autism Manual. She is the author and founder of the Memory series which is a series of social story fiction books from toddlers to teenagers. She enjoys reading and watching movies when she is not writing. Her author website is located at www.toyboxunlimited.com.

CPSIA information can be obtained
at www.ICGtesting.com
Printed in the USA
BVHW03s2156120818
524315BV00001B/31/P